OXFORD

CHORAL
CLASSICS

# Opera Choruses

## EDITED BY JOHN RUTTER

ASSOCIATE EDITOR
**CLIFFORD BARTLETT**

# OXFORD
## UNIVERSITY PRESS

Great Clarendon Street, Oxford OX2 6DP, England
198 Madison Avenue, New York, NY10016, USA

Oxford University Press is a department of the University of Oxford.
It furthers the University's aim of excellence in research, scholarship,
and education by publishing worldwide in

Oxford  New York
Auckland  Bangkok  Buenos Aires  Cape Town  Chennai
Dar es Salaam  Delhi  Hong Kong  Istanbul  Karachi  Kolkata
Kuala Lumpur  Madrid  Melbourne  Mexico City  Mumbai  Nairobi
São Paulo  Shanghai  Taipei  Tokyo  Toronto

Oxford is a registered trade mark of Oxford University Press
in the UK and in certain other countries

15th Impression

ISBN  978-0-19-343693-0

Music originated on Sibelius

Printed in Great Britain on acid-free paper by
Halstan & Co. Ltd., Amersham, Bucks.

Orchestral scores and parts are available on rental
(see the Index of vocal and instrumental requirements on p. 370)

Also available: *Oxford Choral Classics: Opera Choruses Pronunciation Guide*
(an audio aid to the pronunciation of foreign language texts from the volume)
Double CD 978-0-19-343700-5

# CONTENTS

*Preface*
*Notes on the choruses*
*Notes on the plots*

# PREFACE

Opera has in recent years been winning new and wider audiences, whose appetite and interest is by no means confined to performances in the opera house. Verdi would perhaps be surprised, but surely delighted, to know that his work is now being enjoyed by massive crowds in football stadiums, parks, and amphitheatres. Choirs and choral societies have undoubtedly been sharing in this new operatic wave, but it has not been easy for them to offer programmes of opera to their audiences, simply because of the difficulty and inconvenience of assembling all the music. Many opera choruses are not available separately in print, or are handicapped by antiquated translations; orchestral scores and parts (which may have to be gleaned from a number of different rental libraries) are all too often the battle-scarred veterans of decades of use and abuse.

In one sense, then, the aim of this collection of thirty-five classic opera choruses is to meet an obvious practical need. Behind this lies a hope that some of the wealth of marvellous choral music hidden within the pages of opera scores will be opened up to choirs and their audiences.

Such is this wealth that it was hard to decide what to leave out of a one-volume collection. (A future volume of light opera choruses will embrace not only Offenbach, Strauss, and Sullivan, but choruses by Smetana, Mussorgsky, Donizetti, and Chabrier, among others.) It seemed to me important that the choruses included should all be effective in concert performance, taken out of their contexts; regrettably this ruled out some fine choral writing, by Gluck and Berlioz, for example—though not the latter's splendid *Roman carnival* scene. Verdi's contribution of nine choruses is the largest from any single composer: one can only marvel at the extraordinary expressive range of his choral writing, from the operetta-ish wit and *élan* of the Matadors' chorus to the stark tragedy of the chorus of Scottish refugees or the epic grandeur of the *Aida* Triumphal scene. Lack of space and the need to preserve a balance of composers crowded out such fine Verdi choruses as 'O Signore, dal tetto natio' from *I Lombardi* and 'Spunta ecco il dì' from *Don Carlos*; I regret their omission. Most of the other music in the book comes from Verdi's century, the heyday of grand opera; more recent operatic choral writing tends not to be separable from its musical and dramatic context. Earlier choruses are perhaps not generally suitable for large choirs, yet this collection would have been the poorer without Purcell's exquisite final chorus from *Dido and Aeneas* and Handel's charming *Alcina* chorus; Mozart is represented by the Priests' chorus from *Die Zauberflöte* and the less familiar but utterly captivating 'Placido è il mar' from *Idomeneo*.

Over twenty of the choruses in this book can be performed without soloists; others require one or more soloists, and I see this as a positive benefit. Solo singers engaged for choral society concerts will be delighted to have the opportunity to air their operatic talents, not only in the choruses where they join forces with the choir but also in any number of arias, duets, and ensembles that can be used to complete the programme of a gala opera night. Along with any soloists, it may well be worth engaging a narrator to introduce the programme, giving the audience some idea of the stories of the operas from which the choruses are taken (brief notes on the plots are given on p. xi).

An index of the resources required for each chorus—solo, choral, and instrumental—is on p. 370; it is hoped that this will be helpful in drawing up programmes to fit the resources available. Twenty-five choruses are for mixed voices, three for women's voices, and seven for men's voices, which makes for possible variety in programming.

A century ago, opera formed an accepted part of choral society and concert repertoire; it is now making a welcome return. My hope is that this collection will help the process of broadening its audience while at the same time bringing delight, and a new experience, to choral singers everywhere.

*Translations*

For the Russian items, which so notably and colourfully enrich this collection, I have been fortunate in being able to use English translations made by the eminent conductor, linguist, and opera scholar David Lloyd-Jones. All other translations are my own, and in preparing them my aims have been fourfold: to be as faithful as possible to the meaning and flavour of the originals; to alter the rhythms of the originals as little as possible; to preserve the rhyme schemes of the originals as far as possible; and to make the English texts as singable as possible, with due consideration for vowel sounds on exposed notes. As every translator knows (or soon finds out), there are frequent occasions when these aims come into conflict and one or other of them has to be sacrificed. I have tried never to sacrifice singability; though in the case of the *Roman carnival* scene the extreme rapidity of the music makes it difficult to devise *any* text that is singable at Berlioz's metronome mark.

I have not sought to render everything into a uniform quasi-modern English. The tone of the original texts of the Chorus of the Hebrew slaves or the Prayer from *Moïse* is elevated, poetic, and semi-biblical; that of the Matadors' chorus from *La traviata* or the Habanera from *Carmen* more colloquial and contemporary. These differences explain why I have freely used archaic language with 'thee' and 'thou' in the former, and some fairly casual present-day expressions in the latter. The two choruses from *Macbeth* were a special case: Piave's text was inspired by Shakespeare, and where I have been able to echo a Shakespearean phrase I have done so.

A note on the Russian transliterations and their pronunciation, provided by David Lloyd-Jones, appears below.

*Piano reductions*

With the exception of the *Mlada* Procession, the *Eugene Onegin* Waltz scene, and the two *Carmen* extracts, where the composers' own piano reductions have been used, all the piano reductions are mine. They have been conceived as playable rehearsal aids for choral society accompanists rather than as two-stave reductions of every last detail of the orchestral scores. Some critics may miss the string sextuplets from the first section of 'Va, pensiero', the triplet semiquavers from the Pilgrims' chorus, or the wrist-paralyzing repeated quavers in the *Roman carnival* scene; but I suspect that all but the most expert pianists will be glad to see these and other difficulties gone, leaving them freer to provide a firm, clear rhythmic support to the choir. In a few cases, where the orchestral doubling of a choral melody would not leave enough fingers free to play an important accompaniment figure (for example, in the Donizetti *Chorus of wedding guests*), I have omitted it from the reduction. Tremolandos, so ubiquitous in nineteenth-century piano reductions though perhaps less acceptable to modern ears, have been severely rationed; and the extended orchestral introductions to the *Mlada* Procession and the *Macbeth* Witches' chorus have not been shown in full (though of course they are complete in the orchestral rental scores and parts).

*Orchestral scores and parts*

Clear, accurate scores and orchestral parts of every item in this book have been newly typeset and are available on rental from the publisher. These scores and parts agree in every detail (including rehearsal letters) with the vocal scores in this book. Parts for stage band, which is extremely unlikely to be used in concert performances, have been eliminated in the Gounod Soldiers' chorus, the Verdi Triumphal scene and the Wagner Bridal chorus; in the case of the Verdi, the band parts have been transferred to the orchestral brass, though the Egyptian trumpet parts are preserved as an option.

It is never to be recommended that an orchestral score be performed with less than its full complement of instruments, yet it should also be remembered that in the nineteenth century all opera houses had a standing orchestra, sometimes of substantial size. Composers wrote for all the players available, possibly in some cases more because they were there than because the music always demanded them. Conductors may feel that there are instruments in some of the choruses in this book which could be omitted if constraints of space or budget make the use of a full complement impossible. This is a matter best left to individual judgement, and I have shown instruments as optional in the index on p. 370 only if they very clearly can be dispensed with in concert performance (for example, the trumpets and timpani in the Bizet *Habanera*, which have only two notes to play).

*Editorial practice*

Arriving at the best musical and verbal text of an opera—or even an extract from an opera—is not always a simple matter. In a frustratingly large number of cases, autograph manuscripts are lost, destroyed in war, or locked in publishers' vaults, unavailable for general examination; and, as the complex publishing history of an opera such as *Carmen* shows, manuscripts (which predate rehearsals, publication, and subsequent revisions) may not always be the most reliable guide to a composer's final intentions. We have for the most part taken as our sources the earliest possible published full and vocal scores, collated with such more recent ones as are in the public domain; for the Coronation scene from *Boris Godunov* we have been able to use David Lloyd-Jones's authoritative edition. We were able to consult manuscript sources for *Dido and Aeneas* and *Alcina*; and Dr Hugh Macdonald generously assisted with a number of queries relating to *Benvenuto Cellini*.

Dynamic markings, especially in voice parts, are in many cases scanty or lacking altogether in the sources. Where we have supplemented them, our additions appear in square brackets (also used for other editorial additions) or are advertised by footnotes. Illogical or redundant dynamics in the sources have mostly been allowed to stand: such markings, where they were not oversights, were intended to guide the performers of an earlier age towards the composer's desired result, as no doubt were Verdi's sometimes extreme, and very likely deliberately exaggerated, markings.

A feature of the choral writing in many nineteenth-century French and Italian opera scores is the absence of designated alto parts. Verdi sometimes simply wrote 'donne' by his female-voice choral staves, and where a division is specified it is often into first and second sopranos. Mostly the second soprano parts suit the range of female altos quite well, but here and there—for example in the *Roman carnival* scene and the March of the toreadors—there are high-lying passages, and in such places I have where possible shown lower alternatives. For the sake of consistency, the lowest female voice-part in all choruses in this book is labelled 'alto', irrespective of original nomenclature. Where female voice-parts are divided into three without indication of whether the middle part is for second sopranos or first altos, I have used my discretion in allotting it to one or the other, but conductors are accustomed in this situation to reassigning voices if necessary in order to achieve the best three-part balance. Where male-voice parts are divided into three, it is the tenors that are generally divided; evidently they were more plentiful in nineteenth-century opera choruses than in twentieth-century choral societies. In many cases the second tenor parts can be reassigned to baritones if it will make for a more equal balance.

Slurs in vocal parts pose a special problem. In present-day publishing style they tend to be used only to indicate that notes within the slur are sung to one syllable, whereas in the nineteenth century they were used in the same way as instrumental slurs, to indicate phrasing. We have not suppressed these phrasal slurs, though we have followed modern editorial practice in beaming groups of quavers and shorter notes instrumentally, putting in concomitant syllabic slurs except where these might be confused with the composer's phrasal slurs. The result is, we believe, the best compromise in terms of fidelity to the original sources and practical legibility to the modern choral singer.

Accurate underlay of Italian texts can be problematic because it frequently happens that more than one syllable is sung to a single note. It is sometimes a moot point which one of a cluster of syllables should be printed directly under a note, which to its left and which to its right; we have attempted to show such clusters in the most readable way.

*Acknowledgements*

It is a pleasure to record here the names of those who have given help and encouragement at various stages of the preparation of this book. My associate editor Clifford Bartlett has given valuable advice on sources and also provided the notes on the opera plots. David Lloyd-Jones and David Sutton have given detailed and extremely helpful scrutiny to the book at proof stage. Dr Hugh Macdonald has shared with me the fruits of his many years of research into Berlioz. Laura Sarti, Ilse Wolf, Anne Champert, Paul Gordon, and David Lloyd-Jones have placed their linguistic expertise at my disposal as I have grappled with Italian, French, German, and Russian texts. Bruce Hamilton has provided the Russian transliterations so essential to non-readers of the Cyrillic alphabet. Jenny Wilson and Brian Clark have ably typeset the orchestral scores and parts. I thank them all.

Of my many friends at Oxford University Press, I especially want to thank Julian Elloway, Senior Music Editor, and Paul Keene, editor for this book, whose interest, support, advice and scrutiny at every stage of the project have been invaluable. Lastly, I gratefully acknowledge the contribution of Ben and Jonathan Finn, inventors of the Sibelius Music Processor, on which the entire book was computer-typeset; their quest for graphical perfection is inspiring.

*JOHN RUTTER*

*Russian transliterations*

Those who have never sung in Russian using a phonetic spelling of the Cyrillic alphabet should not be discouraged from attempting it. In fact, Russian sounds are surprisingly similar to those found in English (though the vowels are largely Italianate), and no attempt at an 'accent' is necessary. Some choirs may be fortunate enough to have a Russian speaker among their members or friends, who can help to perfect what a transliteration can only broadly suggest. The following remarks have therefore been kept to a minimum in the hope that the undertaking will not appear too daunting.

1. The most 'foreign' sound in Russian is the so-called 'hard i'. Here it is represented by 'yi' as in 'Kryilyahk' (*Polovtsian dances*, bar 15). This is pronounced not forward, like the usual English 'i', but backward with an almost adenoidal sound. The main thing is to avoid pronouncing 'yi' as the usual 'i'; try to keep it dark and covered.

2. Clusters of consonants can look intimidating but need not be so. The sound 'kh' is the guttural 'ch' as found in the Scottish word 'loch'; 'zh' is the voiced version of 'sh' and sounds as the 'j' in French 'je'; 'shch' sounds as in 'Engli*sh ch*urch'.

3. The letter 'o' in a pre-stressed syllable (shown in this book as ŏ) is so modified and lightened that it is best pronounced as an 'a' (i.e. 'Barís' for 'Boris'). The letter 'o' in any other unstressed position is pronounced like the 'a' in 'sofa'.

4. Some Russian words, usually verbs, end with a 't' followed by a 'soft sign'. This so softens the 't' that in practice it sounds like 'ts'. In such cases the 's' is shown in brackets. Otherwise, soft signs in Russian have been ignored as most English speaking is soft anyway.

5. The letter 's' in the middle of words has usually been represented by 'ss' in order to prevent it being mispronounced as a 'z' (i.e. 'Mussorgsky' and not the regularly mispronounced 'Muzorgsky').

*DAVID LLOYD-JONES*

# NOTES ON THE CHORUSES

**Beethoven: *Fidelio*, Prisoners' chorus**
First performance 20 November 1805, Vienna (Theater an der Wien) with the title *Leonore*; extensively revised in 1806 and 1814. Vocal dynamic markings have been supplied by reference to Beethoven's fairly explicit orchestral dynamics. The solo/semi-chorus passage in bar 74 (probably intended for tenor because of the clef used) is marked 'Einer oder einige von ihnen' [one or several of them]; the solo in bar 102 (probably for bass) is indicated 'solo'. Rightly or wrongly, the tempo of this chorus in performance is by tradition slower than Beethoven's marking of *Allegro, ma non troppo* might suggest: speeds as slow as ♪ = 80 are not uncommonly encountered.

**Berlioz: *Benvenuto Cellini*, Roman carnival**
First performance 10 September 1838, Paris (Opéra); subsequently revised. The extract given is a self-contained episode within a longer finale; the *Animato* marking at the beginning is, in the original, *A tempo 1° un poco più animato*, the '*tempo 1°*' being *Andantino non troppo lento* (♩ = 76) at the start of the finale. For performances by large choirs conductors may wish to augment the three tenors and three basses specified for the chorus of mountebanks; on the other hand, as their music is not easy, it may be more effective and practical to use only six singers (who can perhaps rehearse in their own time), placed in front of the choir like soloists. Berlioz's score calls for four bassoons; in this edition they have been reduced to two with only the most minimal changes.

**Bizet: *Carmen*, Habanera; March of the toreadors**
First performance 3 March 1875, Paris (Opéra-Comique). Bizet adapted the melody of the Habanera from a song, *El arreglito*, by the Spanish composer Iradier. In the March of the toreadors the part for children's chorus could be taken by a semi-chorus of sopranos if children's choir is unavailable.

**Borodin: *Prince Igor*, Polovtsian dances**
First performance (posthumous) 4 November 1890, St Petersburg (Maryinsky Theatre). The bass solo at bar 151 is rarely sung in concert performances, and can be omitted without loss as the melodic line is already in the orchestra.

**Donizetti: *Lucia di Lammermoor*, Chorus of wedding guests**
First performance 26 September 1835, Naples (San Carlo). The gaiety and high spirits of this chorus make it an obvious winner in performance; in the opera it affords a last moment of lightness before tragedy takes over.

**Gounod: *Faust*, Soldiers' chorus**
First performance 19 March 1859, Paris (Théâtre-Lyrique), with subsequent revisions. Gounod originally wrote the Soldiers' chorus for an abortive opera on Ivan the Terrible. A passage of recitative between bars 103 and 104 has been omitted in our edition. In the original there is a part for stage band which, with only the most minor

exceptions, doubles parts already covered in the orchestra; it has been omitted in our orchestral scores and parts.

**Handel: *Alcina*, Chorus of enchanted islanders**
First performance 16 April 1735, London (Covent Garden). Handel wrote two completely different settings of this chorus, and this one may not have been performed: perhaps its gavotte rhythm was too similar to the final chorus. Its theme is more familiar in its purely instrumental guise as the first movement of Handel's F major Organ Concerto, op .4 no. 4, which appeared in the same year as the opera. Handel's manuscript shows signs of haste, and the third beat of bar 57 presents a puzzle: the violin parts clearly have As, against Gs in the alto, second oboe, and first horn. Either G or A would fit over the bass C (though A is more likely, since it forms a more exact sequence with the two previous bars), but the six-five clash created by both notes together is most uncharacteristic. I have decided to leave the string parts unaltered but to change the alto/oboe/horn G to A.

The tessitura of the tenor part is high at modern pitch, and conductors may want to consider assigning it to altos, with divided sopranos singing the soprano and alto lines, and tenors singing in unison with the basses.

**Leoncavallo: *Pagliacci*, Bell chorus**
First performance 21 May 1892, Milan (Teatro dal Verme), conducted by Toscanini. Dynamic markings in this score are sparse, and have been editorially supplemented. The orchestral score includes a part for church bells on-stage; despite the title of the chorus, these can be omitted. Bars 127–8 are for an on-stage oboe, which is reassigned in this edition to orchestral oboe. The metronome marking of ♩ = 116 for the main section of the chorus is not found in all sources, but is surely right; it is a pity to rush this pastorally charming music, as often seems to happen in performance.

**Mascagni: *Cavalleria rusticana*, Easter hymn**
First performance 17 May 1890, Rome (Teatro Costanzi). The absence of virtually all vocal dynamic markings and the sparseness even of orchestral markings in this score can only leave editors and conductors guessing as to the gifted but inexperienced composer's intentions (*Cavalleria rusticana* was his first and only real success, entered for a competition got up by the Milan publisher Sonzogno). In stage performances choir 2, being off-stage in the church, is likely to sound muted, and this inbuilt dynamic contrast with choir 1, on-stage in the square outside, was perhaps as much subtlety as Mascagni was aiming for. Choir 2 second sopranos in the *Regina cœli* are labelled 'popolo' in the score, indicating that they represent the congregation; in concert performance it might make sense for their responses of 'alleluja' to be sung by choir 1 in unison. If possible, choir 1 and choir 2 should be placed antiphonally. The alto soloist is only included for visual effect, and her part is better omitted in concert performance. A recitative-like conversational exchange between Santuzza

and Alfio, heard over the organ introduction, has been omitted. An English translation of the *Regina cœli* has been provided, but performance in Latin is preferable.

### Mozart: *Die Zauberflöte*, Priests' chorus

First performance 30 September 1791, Vienna (Theater auf der Wieden).

### Mozart: *Idomeneo*, Voyagers' chorus

First performance 29 January 1781, Munich (Hoftheater). The orchestral score and parts of the present edition show the first four bars as an optional introduction, to enable the choir to pitch their first entry.

### Mussorgsky: *Boris Godunov*, Coronation scene

First performance 8 February 1874, St Petersburg (Maryinsky Theatre). The edition of the complete opera from which this scene is extracted is edited by David Lloyd-Jones; it preserves the composer's original version (including its orchestration), removing Rimsky-Korsakov's 'improvements'. From bar 20, where the curtain rises, the score calls for 'a great peal of bells on stage'; these continue until bar 47, resume from bars 91–111, and again from bar 146 till the end of the scene. Orchestral tubular bells scarcely do justice to the majesty of Russian cathedral bells, and conductors may want to investigate the possibilities of appropriate pre-recordings. In the absence of any available bells, bars 39 and 150–1 should be cut to avoid long silences. In bar 85, fourth beat, the second of the two 1st alto quavers is not a misprint: A is correct, not the more likely C, as in the accompaniment. The melody sung by the chorus starting at bar 50 is an old Russian folk-song.

### Puccini: *Madama Butterfly*, Humming chorus

First performance 17 February 1904, Milan (La Scala). The viola d'amore playing on-stage does no more than double the choral melody, to add colour and help the singers maintain pitch; it is generally omitted in concert performances.

### Purcell: *Dido and Aeneas*, Dido's lament, and final chorus

First known performance 1689, London, at 'Josias Priest's Boarding-School at Chelsey by young gentlewomen', but it may have been performed previously at the English court. The use of a ground bass and of a descending fourth are traditional features of Italian laments, whether for lost love or at death. Purcell's notation implies a much slower tempo to the modern musician than it would have done at the time, when triple time was often written in longer notes than duple time. It is best felt as a very slow one-in-a-bar. Crotchet upbeats may be delayed and sung shorter than notated if the tempo is slow enough for that not to sound jerky. In the chorus, the use of ¢ , not C , is significant. The inconsistently notated rhythms on the word 'your' in bar 77 and on the syllable '-ver' in bar 81 should be made to agree.

### Rimsky-Korsakov: *Mlada*, Procession of the nobles

First performance 1 November 1892, St Petersburg (Maryinsky Theatre). The large orchestral forces called for in this dazzling Russian showpiece do not, strictly speaking, include any redundant or optional instruments, but in practice the auxiliary woodwind, horns 4, 5, and 6, and the harp, may possibly be omitted.

### Rossini: *Moïse*, Prayer

First performance 26 March 1827, Paris (Opéra). This fine *bel canto* piece was a great favourite in the nineteenth century, both in its original Italian version, 'Dal tuo stellato soglio', and in the present later French adaptation. A full quartet of soloists is designated to sing with the chorus, but as one of the two female soloists (Anaï) has no solo of her own, her participation is not essential in a concert performance. The double-bass note in bars 51 and 55 is given as D in early sources; this has been changed to F♯ to agree with the vocal bass.

### Rossini: *Guillaume Tell*, Villagers' chorus

First performance 3 August 1829, Paris (Opéra). In the opera this charming chorus follows the celebrated overture, which could effectively precede it in a concert performance also. The stage directions paint a rustic picture of Swiss peasants going about their daily tasks and preparing for wedding celebrations, with the Schachtenthal Falls in the background.

### Tchaikovsky: *Eugene Onegin*, Chorus of peasant girls; Waltz scene

First performance 29 March 1879, Moscow (Mali Theatre), given by students of the Imperial College of Music. Surprisingly, in view of the delicacy of its orchestral colouring, Tchaikovsky's only vocal markings in the Chorus of peasant girls are a *forte* at the opening and a *piano* in bar 95. Conductors may want to add further nuances.

The Waltz scene presents a dilemma in concert performance. The orchestra has the leading melodic role, and the solo contributions of Lensky and Onegin are musically incidental, relating to the development of the plot. If they are included they can seem tantalizing, but if they are omitted the music becomes a little over-repetitive. The suggested cut is a possible solution.

### Verdi: *Il trovatore*, Anvil chorus; Soldiers' chorus

First performance 19 January 1853, Rome (Teatro Apollo). The anvils struck on-stage by the chorus men can in concert performance be taken by the orchestral percussionist(s).

### Verdi: *La traviata*, Brindisi; Matadors' chorus

First performance 6 March 1853, Venice (La Fenice). In the Brindisi, an early vocal score gives *forte* as the dynamic for the start of the introduction; later scores give *piano*, which is generally disregarded in performance. A genuine *piano* (followed, moreover, by *pianississimo*) is hard to reconcile with the gaiety of the party on stage, but if *piano* is correct, Verdi may have been warning the orchestra against playing crudely: Violetta's milieu is one of elegance and sophistication, and the vocal markings *con grazia* and *legerissimo* emphasize that this is no coarse drinking-song but a graceful tribute to youth, beauty, and pleasure.

The soloists in the Matadors' chorus are there simply

because the characters are on-stage. In concert performance there is no reason to include them. As in the Anvil
chorus, there is an instrumental contribution from the
singers: the sopranos and altos (partygoers dressed as
gypsies) are directed to strike tambourines on the first beat
of each bar from bar 153 to the end, and those of the
tenors and basses who are dressed as picadors similarly
thump their lances on the ground between bars 86 and
101, and again from bar 153.

### Verdi: *Nabucco*, Chorus of the Hebrew slaves
First performance 9 March 1842, Milan (La Scala). The
fact that Verdi could have notated this celebrated and
inspiring chorus in 12/8 but chose 4/4 should be taken as a
signal that the dotted rhythms in the chorus part are to be
sung as written and not assimilated into the orchestral
triplets. All vocal slurs are Verdi's own; no syllabic slurs
have been added.

### Verdi: *Macbeth*, Chorus of Scottish refugees; Witches' chorus
First performance of original version 14 May 1847,
Florence (Teatro della Pergola). Revised version first
performed 1865 in Paris. The Refugees' chorus, one of
Verdi's finest choral utterances, has as its theme the plight
of an oppressed country and its people (as does the
Hebrew slaves' chorus); clearly no subject touched the
patriotic composer's heart more deeply. The Witches'
chorus makes an atmospheric opening to the first act of
the opera; explicit instructions for thunder and lightning
are written into the score of the introduction as three
covens of witches appear.

### Verdi: *La forza del destino*, Rataplan
First performance 10 November 1862, St Petersburg
(Bolshoi Theatre). The *forte* chord at the start of this
chorus (necessary to give the pitch) is taken from the
previous bar in the opera, where it concludes a recitative.
Preziosilla is directed to mimic the actions of drumming
(she wears a real military drum), and the word 'rataplan'
is itself intended as an imitation of the sound of a snare
drum. On the final 'pim' in bar 96, everyone is directed to
mime the firing of rifles.

### Verdi: *Aida*, Triumphal scene
First performance 24 December 1871, Cairo (Opera
House). The ballet music which follows bar 134 has been
omitted in this edition. In view of the unlikelihood of a
stage band being used in concert performances, the stage
band part (shown by Verdi only in the form of a two-stave
reduction) has been transferred to the orchestral brass.

### Wagner: *Lohengrin*, Bridal chorus
First performance 28 August 1850, Weimar (Grossher-
zogliches Hoftheater), conducted by Liszt. This chorus
follows directly on from the act 3 Prelude, which would
make a good concert item to precede it. In the original
there is a part for stage band (consisting of 3fl, 2ob, 2cl,
2bsn, 4hn, 2tpt, triangle, and harp) which has been
transferred to the main orchestra in this edition. To those
people who associate Wagner's chorus with religious

wedding ceremonies, it may come as a surprise that it is
sung in the opera as the bridal pair are escorted by their
retinue into the bridal chamber. No amount of bending
Wagner's text in translation will make it fit a church
wedding, and it must be accepted that the piece cannot
appropriately be sung in such a context.

### Wagner: *Tannhäuser*, Pilgrims' chorus
First performance 19 October 1845, Dresden (Hoftheater); revised version, Paris 1861. In order to detach this
chorus from its context in the opera, some alterations have
to be made. The ten bars of introduction originally
included a solo line for Wolfram (bass), which has been
transferred to the orchestra in this edition. Incidental solo
voice-parts (a dialogue between Elisabeth and Wolfram)
have been omitted in bars 16–23, and transferred to the
orchestra in bars 26–32. At bar 78, the music makes an
interrupted cadence leading into a partial reprise of the
chorus, fading away into the distance as the pilgrims
disappear. A simple final cadence of E flat has been
inserted in the orchestra instead: in a stage performance or
recording a fadeout is easily contrived, but is impossible in
a concert performance.

### Wagner: *Die Meistersinger von Nürnberg*, Procession and chorale
First performance 21 June 1868, Munich (Hoftheater).
Only minor alterations are necessary at the start and end
of this magnificent episode in the opera in order to detach
it for concert use. The string chord at the opening, which
originally comes as the end of a continuous busy passage,
has been respaced to correspond with that at the start of
the act 1 prelude (with which the Procession of the
Mastersingers is closely concurrent). At the end of the
extract a final C major cadence has been added and a
*diminuendo* removed, again to make the music correspond
with the prelude.

### Wagner: *Der fliegende Holländer*, Sailors' chorus; Spinning chorus
First performance 2 January 1843, Dresden (Hofoper),
with subsequent revisions. Wagner wrote that the theme
of the Sailors' chorus was suggested to him by the singing
of sailors he had heard in Norway in 1839. I have used
the splendid old nautical word 'sailorman' to translate
'Steuermann' in preference to 'steersman' or 'helmsman'
because it seems to me important that each of the three
notes should have its own syllable, to match the *staccato*
orchestral articulation. Conductors should, however, feel
free to revert to either of the other two terms.
   In the Spinning chorus, a passage of soloists' dialogue in
between the two verses has been omitted.

### Weber: *Der Freischütz*, Huntsmen's chorus
First performance 18 June 1821, Berlin. Early editions of
the opera disagree about whether there is a tie in bar 1
(and all parallel places) between the crotchet and the first
of the four semiquavers. I have adopted the reading
without a tie on the grounds that it matches the vocal
articulation.

# NOTES ON THE PLOTS

## Beethoven: *Fidelio*

The opera is set in the eighteenth century, in a fortress near Seville. The author of the original libretto, J.-N. Bouilly, claimed it was based on a true story. It had already been set by three composers before Beethoven's version was performed. His opera has come to symbolize not only the desire for and achievement of freedom from tyranny but also the power of conjugal love. Florestan is secretly imprisoned by the wicked Pizarro. Florestan's wife Leonora disguises herself as a man (under the name Fidelio) and gets a job as assistant to the chief gaoler (Rocco). Pizarro fears an inspection of the prison from Don Fernando, a senior member of the government, so decides to kill Florestan, but the trumpet-call announcing Fernando's arrival comes just as Leonora reveals her identity and dares Pizarro to kill her as well. All ends happily, except for Pizarro. The chorus of prisoners occurs towards the end of the first of the two acts; at Leonora's request, the prisoners are allowed into the courtyard in honour of the king's birthday. Their delight in their temporary freedom is a foretaste of the general rejoicing at the end of the opera.

## Berlioz: *Benvenuto Cellini*

The life of Benvenuto Cellini is known more intimately than that of most other Renaissance artists, thanks to his racy autobiography. This provides the background for Berlioz's opera, which is set in Rome in 1532 on the evening before Shrove Tuesday as Carnival approaches its height. The plot concerns Cellini's scheme to disguise himself as a monk and elope with Teresa, the papal treasurer's daughter. This goes seriously awry, and a man gets killed; but Cellini ultimately wins her because of the beauty of his new statue of Perseus (the libretto does not explain how it happens to be in Rome rather than Florence). The Carnival scene closes the second of the three acts, with crowds coming to see the *commedia dell'arte* show. Berlioz based much of his concert overture *Le carnaval romain* on the music of this scene.

## Bizet: *Carmen*

*Carmen* is based on a short novel by Prosper Mérimée. It is set in Seville in about 1820. Don José, a corporal in the dragoons, is in love with a nice, pretty girl, Micaela, but their relationship is broken up by a wild gypsy beauty, Carmen, who entices him to run off with her and join the smugglers in the mountains. Carmen soon tires of him and her fancy then turns to the bullfighter Escamillo. Don José confronts Carmen outside the arena during a bullfight. Carmen exults when she hears the crowd acclaiming Escamillo's victory. Don José stabs her and gives himself up as the crowds pour out of the arena. The Habanera is Carmen's first attempt to entice Don José; it is sung as the girls emerge from the cigarette factory where they work, and introduces her to the audience. The March of the toreadors sets the scene for the bullfight at the end of the opera. The *alguazil*, who heads the parade in the costume of a sixteenth-century bailiff, is chief official; the *chulos* are assistant bullfighters who act as seconds to the principal matador; the *banderilleros* stick decorated staves into the bull's neck; the *picadors*, on horseback, further weaken the bull's neck muscle with lances; the *espada* is the principal bullfighter who finally kills the bull.

## Borodin: *Prince Igor*

Borodin was by profession a chemist and was able to compose only in his spare time. He worked for eighteen years on *Prince Igor*, but it was incomplete at his death and was finished by Rimsky-Korsakov and Glazunov. The *Polovtsian dances*, however, were completed and orchestrated by Borodin himself. The libretto, by the composer, is based on an old Russian chronicle and relates to an incident in 1185, at a time of conflict between Russia and the Tartars. Igor, prince of Seversk, is defeated by Khan Konchak of the Polovtsi, who holds him as an honoured and respected captive. The dances at the end of act 2 are performed by the slave dancers of the Khan to entertain Prince Igor.

## Donizetti: *Lucia di Lammermoor*

The novels of Sir Walter Scott exerted an enormous influence on European culture in the second quarter of the nineteenth century, and this is reflected in a large number of operas. *Lucia di Lammermoor* is drawn from *The bride of Lammermoor* and is set near Edinburgh around 1700. Lucia has been promised in marriage to the wealthy Arturo by her impoverished brother Enrico, but she is already in love with Edgaro, who is travelling in France on a diplomatic mission. Enrico produces a forged letter implying that Edgaro has been unfaithful, so Lucia agrees reluctantly to the wedding. 'Per te d'immenso giubilo' introduces the signing of the nuptial documents. Edgaro appears just as the signing is completed and a dramatic sextet follows. The famous mad scene is in the last act after Lucia has killed her husband.

## Gounod: *Faust*

Gounod's opera on the Faust legend, set in sixteenth-century Germany, concentrates primarily on a theme introduced by Goethe. The aged philosopher Faust is enticed by the vision of a young and beautiful woman, Marguerite, to accept the gift of youth offered by Méphistophélès. Faust sees her walking home from church, then courts her indirectly by offering a casket of jewels provided by Méphistophélès; she responds with the famous Jewel Song. They fall in love but he deserts her. Guiltily pregnant, she goes to church to pray, but Méphistophélès convinces her that she is doomed. The soldiers return from war and, in 'Déposons les armes', sing of victory. The scene leads to a brawl in which Faust kills Marguerite's brother. She is imprisoned for killing her child. Faust visits her, but she invokes the angels rather than escape with him.

## Handel: *Alcina*

This is one of three operas Handel wrote in the 1730s on librettos deriving from Ariosto's *Orlando furioso*. Alcina is an enchantress who entices heroes into her domain to become her lovers, transforming them into rocks, streams, trees or wild beasts. The chorus comes at the beginning of the opera and is sung by her captives after her palace has dramatically appeared from the middle of a mountain.

## Leoncavallo: *Pagliacci*

The opera is set in Calabria in the 1860s and involves interplay between the dramatic activity of a group of *commedia dell'arte* players and their real emotions, played out before a village audience. The Bell chorus is an interlude sung by villagers as the church bells announce Vespers.

## Mascagni: *Cavalleria rusticana*

This has become an inseparable double-bill companion of *Pagliacci*, both operas sharing a concern with what was at the time considered a realistic portrayal of rural life. The term *verismo* was used particularly in connection with the author Giovanni Verga, and *Cavalleria rusticana* is based on a short novel by him. The action takes place in the present (i.e. 1890) in a village in Sicily. The story of the opera is one of love, betrayal, and death, and the function of the Easter hymn is to provide local colour and show the religious devotion which is another side of the hot-blooded Sicilian character.

## Mozart: *Die Zauberflöte*

Mozart's last opera is a mixture of fairy story and pantomime with an imaginative portrayal of masonic ritual and symbolism. Tamino and Pamina are led through a series of trials before they are allowed to marry. The opera is set in Egypt, and the hieratic aspects of the story are directed by Sarastro, the high priest of Isis and Osiris. 'O Isis und Osiris' is sung to introduce the lovers' trial by fire and water.

## Mozart: *Idomeneo*

Idomeneo is delayed by storms on his voyage back to Crete after the Trojan War and vows that, if Neptune grant that he reaches home, he will sacrifice the first person he meets there. That person turns out to be his son Idamante. Idomeneo tries to escape from the consequences by sending him away, and 'Placido è il mar' is sung as Idamante is about to depart with the Greek princess Elettra (who loves him, though he prefers the Trojan princess Ilia). Another storm forces Idomeneo to carry out his vow, but he is reprieved by Neptune at the last moment, provided that he abdicates in favour of his son and his son's bride-to-be Ilia.

## Mussorgsky: *Boris Godunov*

The opera has a complicated history; there are two versions by the composer, one in seven scenes, the other in a prologue and four acts. Until the last few years it was generally performed in a revision by Rimsky-Korsakov. Boris, a member of the Russian imperial family by marriage, has contrived the death of the rightful heir to the throne, the tsarevich Dimitri, and has become tsar. The opera concerns Boris's struggle with his conscience and the rise to power of a young monk Grigori, who claims to be the murdered Dimitri. The prologue has two scenes. The first shows the Russian people confused by events, the second (included here complete) is the coronation of Boris at the Kremlin in 1598.

## Puccini: *Madama Butterfly*

The opera, based on an allegedly true incident turned into a play by the American dramatist David Belasco, is set in Nagasaki. An American naval officer, Pinkerton, has enticed a Japanese geisha, Butterfly, to marry him. Duty soon takes him away, and when he returns three years later, he has an American wife. Butterfly is told this, but cannot believe it. The Humming Chorus is sung as the moon shines into her bedroom while she and her child sleep. Next day the truth becomes clear to her and, broken-hearted, she kills herself.

## Purcell: *Dido and Aeneas*

After besieging Troy for ten years, the Greeks finally enter the city (by means of a wooden horse) and sack it. The Trojan prince Aeneas escapes, under the protection of Venus, who intends that he should found a new city in Italy: Rome. On the way, his ship is driven by storms to Carthage, where the widowed queen, Dido, is immediately drawn to him. Aeneas is tempted to stay, and is only tricked into fulfilling his destiny by a sorceress and her associates. Dido is heartbroken. Imperiously dismissing the vacillating Aeneas, she sings her lament and dies. (Her song is addressed to her companion, Belinda: it is Belinda that Dido does not want to trouble, not Aeneas.)

## Rimsky-Korsakov: *Mlada*

Described by its composer as a 'magic opera-ballet', *Mlada*, the fourth of his fifteen operas, is very much a pretext for displaying pageantry, ballet sequences, and scenic effects; in fact, acts 2 and 3 consist of little else. It is set in Retra, city-state of the Polabians or Baltic Slavs. Mlada herself is one of the rare non-singing title-roles in opera, for before the action begins she has been murdered by Voislava, daughter of Prince Mstivoi, who desires Yaromir, Mlada's husband. In the fourth act the ghosts of Yaromir's ancestors inform him of Voislava's crime. He kills her, and after he and the whole city have been destroyed by flood and earthquake he and Mlada are seen reunited in a final apotheosis. The Procession of the nobles takes place at the beginning of act 2 when the Polabian princes assemble at a national festival.

## Rossini: *Moïse*

Rossini's French opera on the story of Moses is based on his Italian sacred drama *Mosè in Egitto*, written to be performed at the Teatro San Carlo in Naples during Lent 1818. The Paris version of nine years later was considerably altered, though the Prayer differs only in its text. It is sung by the Children of Israel as they are trapped between the Egyptian army and the Red Sea.

### Rossini: *Guillaume Tell*

The opera is set in Switzerland in the thirteenth century and is based on a famous play by Schiller. The Swiss are smarting under the rule of the Austrian governor Gesler; eventually he is shot by William Tell with the second of two arrows (the first of which has shot the famous apple from his son's head) and the Swiss gain their freedom. 'Quel jour serein' opens the opera and sets the scene.

### Tchaikovsky: *Eugene Onegin*

Tchaikovsky himself did most of the work to adapt Pushkin's classic poem as a libretto, preserving much of the original text. The opening is set on a country estate in the 1820s. Tatyana falls in love with the worldly Onegin and writes him a passionate letter. The following scene, the Chorus of peasant girls, takes place in the garden; a group of girls sing while they gather berries. Tatyana and Onegin meet; he says he is not inclined for marriage. Act 2 is set at a ball in honour of Tatyana's name-day. The guests are dancing a waltz, expressing their enjoyment and gossiping. After the waltz Onegin quarrels with his friend Lensky. They fight a duel and Lensky is killed. Some years later Onegin returns from self-imposed exile and meets Tatyana, who is now married, in St Petersburg. He falls in love with her; Tatyana says that she still loves him, but is loyal to her husband. A particular feature of the opera is the way the story develops against a background of dance music.

### Verdi: *Il trovatore*

The opera is set in Spain in the early fifteenth century and is based on a play by Antonio Garcia Gutiérrez that had been an immediate success in 1836. The plot is complex, and the two choruses in this book do not depend on detailed knowledge of it. The Anvil chorus opens act 2: gypsies (who earn their living as tinkers) are striking their anvils and singing in praise of the approaching dawn and the pleasures of work, wine, and women. The Soldiers' chorus comes near the beginning of act 3 as the troops are told they will assault the enemy next day.

### Verdi: *La traviata*

The opera is based on the novel by Alexandre Dumas *La dame aux camélias* (1848), which Verdi had seen in its stage version in 1852. Dumas gave a modern Parisian setting to his partly autobiographical work. The opera opens with a party at the house of a fashionable courtesan, Violetta. Alfredo, in love with her, sings the Brindisi (an alternation between a soloist, who calls on the company to raise their glasses, and a choral response), which is taken up by the chorus and repeated by Violetta. Their love develops, she abandons her former life, and they set up home together. But Alfredo's father persuades her to leave him, since the scandal of the liaison is preventing the marriage of Alfredo's sister. Violetta writes to Alfredo saying she is returning to her old life. At another party, in act 2, friends of Alfredo turn up dressed as matadors and sing of their fearless life, gambling with fortune. When Alfredo arrives, Violetta lies that she loves her new protector. In act 3, Alfredo realizes the true nature of her sacrifice but it is too late: Violetta dies of consumption.

### Verdi: *Nabucco*

Verdi wrote in 1879 that he was given the libretto for *Nabucco* (after it had been rejected by Nicolai) and when he looked at it, it fell open at 'Va, pensiero'. The opera's triumphant success was due at least in part to the melody to which he set this paraphrase of psalm 137. It is recounted that all the stage-hands at the first run of performances would gather every night in the wings to hear the great chorus. It is sung by the Israelites as they lament the loss of their homeland, and was soon widely interpreted as a political gesture, becoming the anthem of Italian patriotism. At Verdi's funeral the crowd spontaneously broke into it. The narrative, which derives from a French play produced in Paris in 1836, is set around the biblical story of the Jews in Babylonian exile in 586 BC.

### Verdi: *Macbeth*

Piave's adaptation of Shakespeare's play is freer than the version of *Othello* made by Boito for Verdi in the 1880s. Verdi himself planned the scenario. The opera was extensively revised for a revival in Paris in 1865. The Witches' chorus opens act 1 and is set in a Scottish wood (Shakespeare's 'blasted heath'). The chorus of Scottish refugees (set in a deserted place on the Anglo-Scottish border, with Birnam Wood—in fact over a hundred miles away—visible in the distance) comes from the 1865 version.

### Verdi: *La forza del destino*

Piave adapted his libretto from a Spanish play, *Don Alvaro o la fuerza del sino*, written in the 1830s; it also incorporates a scene from Schiller's *Wallensteins Lager* which portrays life in a military camp. It is set in Spain and Italy in the middle of the eighteenth century. The Rataplan comes towards the end of act 3 (at the very end of act 3 in the 1869 revision). The soldiers are upset by a friar who preaches at them, and start beating him up, but Preziosilla, a young gypsy camp-follower, brings them to order by starting a song with drum accompaniment.

### Verdi: *Aida*

The Khedive of Egypt tried to get a new opera from Verdi for the opening of the Cairo Opera House and the Suez Canal in 1869, but had to be content with an existing work, *Rigoletto*. Two years later Verdi did give Cairo their new opera, *Aida*; the idea came from a noted Egyptologist, Auguste Mariette. The action is set in Egypt during the time of the Pharaohs, and, despite the local colour, uses situations familiar from countless opera plots. It includes a magnificent march and series of dances in honour of the king, providing a massive scene of state pomp before the private tragedy which takes up the rest of the opera.

### Wagner: *Lohengrin*

The opera is set in Antwerp in the early tenth century. Elsa has been promised in marriage to a mysterious knight as his reward for championing her. She, however, is disturbed by his condition that she must never ask him his true name or origin. The wedding celebrations begin act 3. After the famous prelude, the curtain rises on an empty bridal chamber. Elsa and Lohengrin are escorted into the chamber to the music of this chorus. Their retinue leaves during the last few bars. Elsa is disquieted by her husband's anonymity and forces him to reveal that he is Lohengrin, son of Parsifal. He returns to Montsalvat, the temple of the Holy Grail, borne away in a boat which had appeared drawn by a swan, now miraculously transformed into Elsa's murdered brother Gottfried, restored to life and proclaimed by the departing Lohengrin as Duke of Brabant.

**Wagner:** *Tannhäuser*

The action of this opera takes place in the early thirteenth century near Eisenach (Bach's future birthplace). The story revolves around the tension between spiritual and erotic love, embodied in a song contest between Wolfram von Eschenbach and Tannhäuser. The Pilgrims' chorus (its theme already heard in the overture) comes in act 3 as a group of aged pilgrims return from Rome.

**Wagner:** *Die Meistersinger von Nürnberg*

Like *Tannhäuser*, this opera is built around a song contest, but set rather later, in the sixteenth century, by which time the tradition of German guild-singers was no longer aristocratic. Two older masters, the cobbler poet Sachs and the town clerk Beckmesser, are confronted by a revolutionary youngster, Walther. The prize at the midsummer song contest is Eva, with whom Walther is passionately in love. Walther wins; the pedantic Beckmesser cannot understand the new style and loses. Sachs recognizes that he is of the older generation (so foregoes winning Eva for himself), but reminds the crowd that the impetuosity of youth needs artistic discipline in order to uphold the tradition of true German art. The procession of the mastersingers is heard in act 3 as the town assembles for the contest; Sachs appears, and the crowd spontaneously acclaims him, breaking into a rendition of one of his compositions, 'Wach auf', a song in praise of the dawn. The text is by the historical Hans Sachs, the dawn referred to being Luther's Reformation.

**Wagner:** *Der fliegende Holländer*

The devil condemned a Dutch captain to sail the oceans until doomsday unless he finds a faithful woman to redeem him. He is allowed to land once every seven years to search for her. On one such occasion, the Dutchman moors in a Norwegian port next to Daland's ship and offers him his treasures if he can be permitted to woo Daland's daughter Senta. Act 2 begins with the Spinning chorus: the women sing while they spin, and as they do so, Senta leans back in an armchair and gazes at a portrait of the mythical Flying Dutchman. After the chorus, she sings a ballad about the myth and is immediately entranced when the person from the picture and story appears in real life. At the beginning of act 3 the Norwegian sailors are merrymaking. The Dutchman hears Senta reject her previous suitor and, fearing that she may also reject him, puts to sea. Senta proclaims her faithfulness and throws herself off a cliff into the sea, but she and the Dutchman are seen in transfigured embrace above the waves as the curtain falls.

**Weber:** *Der Freischütz*

*Der Freischütz* embodies the German romantic love of the forest and the mysterious (sometimes sinister) power of nature. There is to be a shooting contest: the winner will marry Agathe, the daughter of the chief forester, and will succeed him. The favoured candidate, Max, is off form. Another forester, Caspar, tempts him to visit the Wolf's Glen, where, under the auspices of Samiel, the Wild Huntsman, they can make seven magic bullets. Six are used for hunting: the seventh goes where Samiel chooses. At the contest, Max accidentally shoots Caspar, but is forgiven and allowed to marry Agathe after a year's penance. Hunting music pervades the opera; the Huntsmen's chorus comes in act 3, shortly before the final denouement.

# 1. Prisoners' chorus

(from *Fidelio*)

Text by J. Sonnleithner and F. Treitschke
tr. John Rutter

L. van BEETHOVEN
(1770–1827)

Note: All vocal dynamic markings in this chorus are editorial, except for those in bars 139–144.

**F** SOLO or SEMI-CHORUS

Wir wol - len mit Ver - trau - en auf Got - tes Hil - fe, auf
*A light still burns in - side us: We trust in God, His*

Got - tes Hil - fe bau - en, die Hoff-nung flü - stert sanft mir zu: Wir wer - den
*strength will help and guide us. I feel new hope a - rise in my breast: We shall be*

frei, wir fin - den Ruh, wir fin - den Ruh.
*free, we shall find rest, we shall find rest.*

TENORS

O Him - mel! Ret - tung!
*O hea - ven! Res - cue!*

BASSES

# 2. Roman carnival

(from *Benvenuto Cellini*)

Text by L. de Wailly and A. Barbier
tr. John Rutter

HECTOR BERLIOZ
(1803–69)

**Animato**

**PIANO**

*f*

*cresc.*

**Presto scherzando** ( ♩. = 152 )

**TENORS** [A] [*f*]

Ve - nez,  ve - nez  peu - ple  de  Ro - me,  Ve - nez  en -
*Roll up,  roll  up,  good  Ro - man  peo - ple,  Roll up  and*

★**CHORUS OF MOUNTEBANKS**

**BASSES**

[*f*]

[A]

*ff*          *f*

*Berlioz specifies three tenors and three basses.

© Oxford University Press 1995. Photocopying copyright material is illegal.

*Berlioz directs the soprano soloist (Teresa) to sing in unison with the 1st sopranos, except in her solo passage (bars 92–100).

39

Sur Ro-me dé-rou-le La joie et le
*The car-ni-val's set-ting all of Rome a-*

Ro-me dé-rou-le La joie et le bruit,
*car-ni-val's set-ting the ci-ty a-light,*

La joie et le
*Set-ting Rome a-*

43   **D**   *poco più f*

bruit,
*-light.*

L'a-mour et l'i-vres-se Dans la
*It goes to your head, and love is*

*mf poco cresc.*

bruit, L'a-mour et l'i-vres-se Dans la ville en feux,
*-light. It goes to your head and there's love in the air,*

*poco più f*

Dans la
*love is*

**D**   *poco più f*

47   *più f*

ville en feux,
*in the air.*

Chas-sent la tris-tes-se
*For-get all your trou-ble,*

*mf*   *cresc. poco*

ville en feux. Chas-sent la tris-tes-se Des cœurs et des yeux,
*in the air. For-get all your trou-ble, for-get all your care,*

*più f*

*mf*   *cresc. poco*   *più f*

Mas-ques noirs, ven-tres ronds, Ve - nez voir les bouf-fons._____
*Come a - long, come a - long, Or you'll all miss your chance._____*

-vons, chan-tons, dan-sons.
*drink and sing and dance.*

Ah!_____
*Ah!_____*

vi - ve la joie, vi - ve la joie Que l'on s'y noie, Bu -
*long__ live__ en-joy-ment, long__ live fun For ev-'ry-one, Let's*

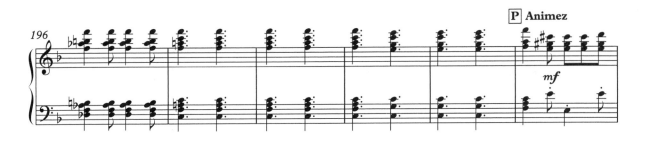

**ROMAN PEOPLE**

L'a- mour et l'i - vres - - se
*To - night is for mad - - ness*

Le car - na - val
*Long live de - - light*

Chas-
*To*

Est
*This*

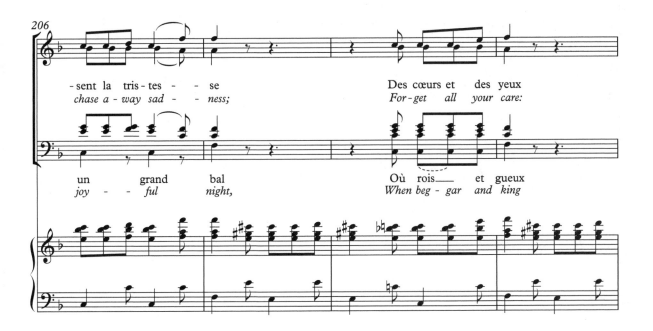

-sent la tris- tes - - se
*chase a - way sad - - ness;*

un grand bal
*joy - - ful night,*

Des cœurs et des yeux
*For - get all your care:*

Où rois— et gueux
*When beg - gar and king*

# 3. Habanera

## (from *Carmen*)

Text by H. Meilhac and L. Halévy
tr. John Rutter

GEORGES BIZET
(1838–75)

\* The piano reduction is Bizet's own.

**20** [A]   *espress.*

plaît.____   L'a - - mour!____   L'a - mour!____
see!____   Ah,   love,____   sweet   love!____

SOPRANOS and ALTOS *unis.* *pp* *legg.*

CHORUS   L'a-mour est un oi-seau re - bel-le Que nul ne   peut ap - pri-voi - ser,   Et c'est
Love's a   bird that will not o - bey,__ A bird too   wild for you to   tame;   If her

TENORS *div.*

[A] *pp* *legg.*

**25**   *p*

L'a - - mour!____   L'a - mour! L'a-mour est
Ah,   love,____   sweet   love! Love knows no

bien en vain qu'on l'ap - pel - le, S'il lui con - vient de_ re - fu - ser!
plea-sure's to stay a - way,__ No use for you to_ call her name!

**29**

en - fant de Bo - hême, Il n'a ja - mais, ja - mais con - nu de   loi, Si tu ne m'ai - mes pas, je
rules and has no   home, A gip-sy wan-der-ing as free as   air; And if my   fan - cy starts to

99

tu  ne  m'ai - mes  pas,  je    t'ai - - me!        Mais si  je  t'ai - me, si  je
*warn- ing  you, young man, take   care!_____     And if   I   want you,  if  I*

Prends garde  à     toi!
*Young  man, take   care!*

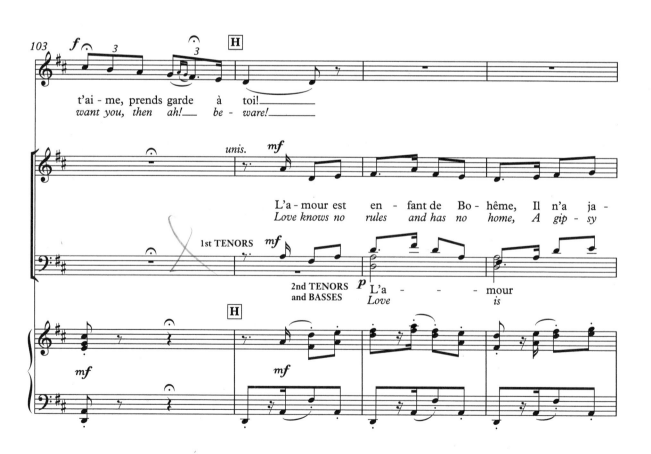

103

t'ai - me, prends garde    à    toi!_____
*want you, then   ah!__ be - ware!_____*

L'a - mour est   en - fant de  Bo - hême,  Il  n'a  ja -
*Love knows no   rules  and has  no  home,  A  gip - sy*

1st TENORS *mf*

2nd TENORS *p* L'a - - - mour
and BASSES   *Love*          *is*

# 4. March of the toreadors

(from *Carmen*)

Text by H. Meilhac and L. Halévy
tr. John Rutter

GEORGES BIZET
(1838–75)

* The piano reduction is Bizet's own.

**TENORS and BASSES**

*Et puis sa - lu - ons au pas - sa - - - ge,  Sa - lu - ons___ les har - dis  Chu -*
*Here come men so no - ble in bear - - ing,  Raise a cheer___ for the bold  Chu -*

*-los!_____    Bra - vo!   vi - va!   gloire  au cou - ra - ge!*
*-los!_____    Bra - vo!   vi - va!   here's  to their dar - ing!*

# 5. Polovtsian dances

### (from *Prince Igor*)

Text by the composer
tr. David Lloyd-Jones

ALEXANDER BORODIN
(1833–87)

U-lye-tai___ na___ kryil-yakh vye-tra___ tyi vkrai rŏd-noi, rŏd-na___-ya pyess-nya
Fly a-way___ on___ gen-tle___ breez-es;___ fly swift-ly,___ songs of love,___ to greet our___

*or sing lower 1st tenor part, with all 1st tenors on upper part.

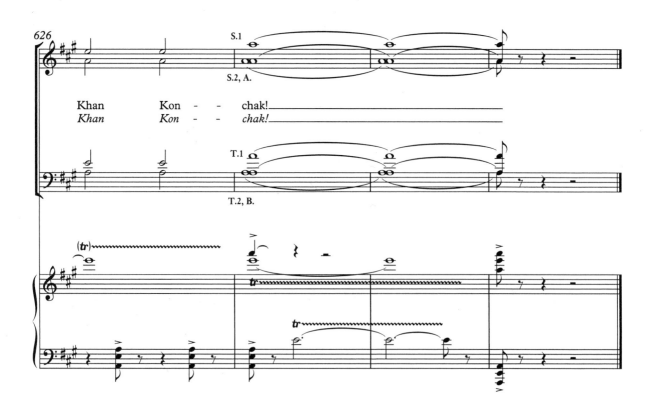

# 6. Chorus of wedding guests

(from *Lucia di Lammermoor*)

Text by S. Cammarano
tr. John Rutter

GAETANO DONIZETTI
(1797–1848)

Per te d'im-men - so giu - bi - lo
*Fill ev - 'ry cup, come ce - le - brate!*

47
-rì la vo-stra stel - - la: io la fa-rò ri - sor- ge-re più
star re-nowned in sto - - ry; Glad-ly I see it rise a-gain to

51
ful - gi-da, più bel - - la. La man mi por-gi En-
great - er light and glo - - ry. In to - - ken give your

54
-ri - co, ti strin - - gi a que-sto cor, a te ne
hand now, This heart of mine is true; I vow be-

57
ven - go a-mi - - -co, fra-tel - lo e di-fen-
-side you I'll stand now as bro - -ther and friend to

fp

116

# 7. Soldiers' chorus

(from *Faust*)

Text by J. Barbier and M. Carré
tr. John Rutter

CHARLES GOUNOD
(1818–93)

Dé - po - sons les ar - mes,
*Com-rades, lay your arms down,*

72

dé - po - sons les ar - mes,  Dans nos_ fo - yers en - fin___ nous voi - ci re - ve-
*Home-ward we're re - turn - ing,*  *Home - ward re - turn - ing now___ that our du - ty is*

77

*espressivo*
*p*

-nus!___  Nos mè - - res en lar - mes,  Nos mè - res et nos sœurs___ ne
*done.___*  *In tears___  and yearn - ing  Our loved ones fond - ly wait___ for*

*p espressivo*

*p*

82

nous at - ten - dront plus.  Dé - po - sons les ar - mes!  Nos mè - res en
*ev - 'ry mo - ther's son.*  *Home - ward we're re - turn - ing,  Our loved ones are*

*cresc.*
*f*  *p*  *f*  *p*

lar - mes, Nos mè - res et nos sœurs ne nous at - ten - dront plus, Nos mè - res et nos
*yearn - ing; Their tears soon will be o - ver now the war is won, Their tears will soon be*

sœurs ne nous at - ten - dront plus.___ Dé - po - sons les
*o - ver now the war is won.___ Com - rades, lay your*

ar - mes, dé - po - sons les ar - mes!
*arms down, Home - ward we're re - turn - - ing!*

D Tempo marziale

Gloire im - mor - tel - le De nos aï - eux____ Sois - nous fi -
*Glo - ry and praise to the men of old;____ We will re -*

- dè - le, Mou-rons comme eux!____ Et sous ton ai - le, Sol-dats vain-queurs, Di-
*- mem-ber their deeds so bold!____ Sol - - diers, we're rea-dy to play our part;____ A*

-ri - ge nos pas,    di - ri - ge nos pas,    en - flam - me nos cœurs!
*spring  in    our  step,    a   spring  in   our  step,    and  fire_____  in   our  heart._____*

Pour  toi  mè - re  pa - tri - e    Af - fron - tant  le  sort_____
*For   the    land  that  we  love_____   we  would  risk   our  all:_____*

Tes    fils    l'âme a - guer - ri - e,  Ont  bra - vé  la  mort._____
*Death  or    glo - ry  we  face_____  at  the  trum - pet's  call._____*

Ta    voix    sain-te    nous    crie:____    En    a-vant,    sol-dats,____    Le
*When    the    cry    is    'Ad-vance!'____    and    the    foe's    in    sight,____    To-*

fer    à    la    main,    le    fer    à    la    main,    Cou-rez____    aux    com-bats!____
*-ge-ther    we'll    stand,    a    sword    in    our    hand,    and    rea--dy    to    fight!____*

Gloire    im-mor-tel-le    De    nos    aï-eux____    Sois-    nous    fi-
*Glo--ry    and    praise    to    the    men    of    old;____    We    will    re-*

160

**ff**

pas!_____ Gloire im - mor - tel - le De nos aï - eux,___
way._____ Glo - - ry and praise to the men of old;___

163

Sois - nous fi - dè - le, Mou-rons comme eux!__ Et sous ton
We will re - mem-ber their deeds so bold!__ Sol - diers, we're

166

ai - le, Sol - dats vain-queurs,__ Di - ri - ge nos pas, en-flam - - me nos
rea - dy to play our part;__ A spring in our step, and fire___ in our

*Alternative ending point here

# 8. Chorus of enchanted islanders

(from *Alcina*)

Text anonymous, after Ariosto
tr. John Rutter

G. F. HANDEL
(1685–1759)

*Small notes here and elsewhere in the bass part are editorial alternatives.

centro del goder, del goder,
*fount of joy and bliss,* *joy and bliss,*

del goder; qui è l'E-li-so de' vi-ven-ti, qui l'e-
*joy and bliss;* *Earth-ly con-tent - ment with-out mea-sure, Ne - ver*

-roi for-ma il pia-cer, qui l'e-roi for-ma il pia-
*such de-light as this,* *Ne - ver such de-light as*

*Alto C, although clear in Handel's ms., may be meant to be an A, the same as bar 54.

cen - tro del go - der,                    del go - der,
*fount of* *joy and* *bliss,*              *joy and* *bliss,*

del go - der,        que - sto è il cen - tro del go - der.
*joy and* *bliss,*   *here the fount of* *joy and bliss.*

# 9. Bell chorus

(from *Pagliacci* )

Text by the composer
tr. John Rutter

RUGGERO LEONCAVALLO
(1857–1919)

*originally, sopranos

# 10. Easter hymn

(from *Cavalleria Rusticana*)

Text by G. Targioni-Tozzetti
and G. Menasci
tr. John Rutter

PIETRO MASCAGNI
(1863–1945)

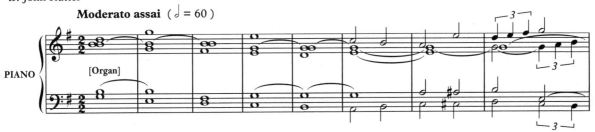

**★CHOIR 2**

*In the opera, Choir 1 is onstage outside the church, Choir 2 offstage inside the church.

Note: Vocal dynamic markings are editorial.

Easter Hymn
Words by Guido Menasci, Giovanni Targioni-Tozzetti and Frederick Weatherly
Music by Pietro Mascagni © 1973 Casa Musicale Sonzogno, Italy. Ascherberg Hopwood & Crew Ltd, London W6 8BS
Reproduced by permission of International Music Publications Ltd
All Rights Reserved.

*This marking is the composer's own.

# 11. Priests' chorus

(from *Die Zauberflöte*)

Text by E. Schikaneder
tr. John Rutter

W. A. MOZART
(1756–91)

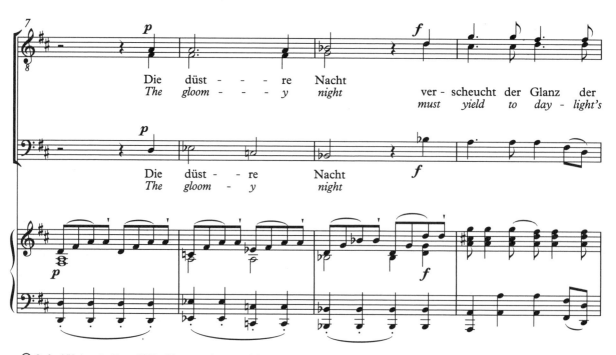

# 12. Voyagers' chorus

(from *Idomeneo*)

Text by G. Varesco
tr. John Rutter

W. A. MOZART
(1756–91)

# 13. Coronation scene

(from *Boris Godunov*)

Words by the composer, after Pushkin
tr. David Lloyd-Jones

MODESTE MUSSORGSKY
(1839–81)

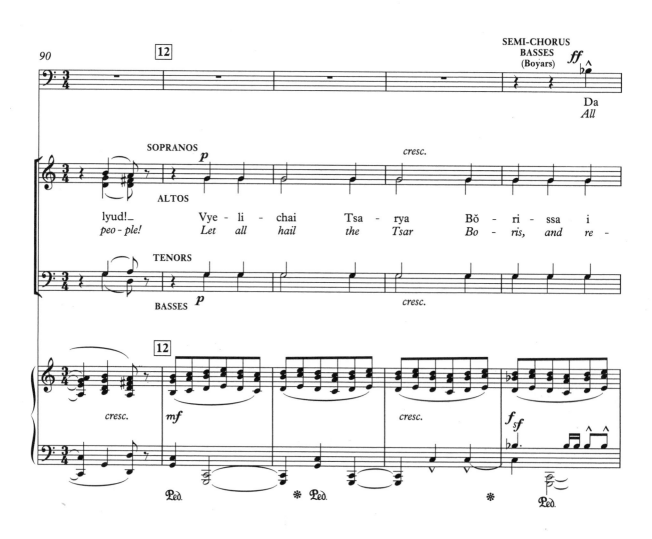

zdrast - vu-yet Tsar    Bŏ - ris Fye - o - do-ro-vich!
*hail    to thee, Tsar    Bo - ris Fe - o - do-ro-vich!*

slav!    Da    zdrast-vu-yet!    Uzh kak
*- joice!    All    hail    to thee!    O - ver*

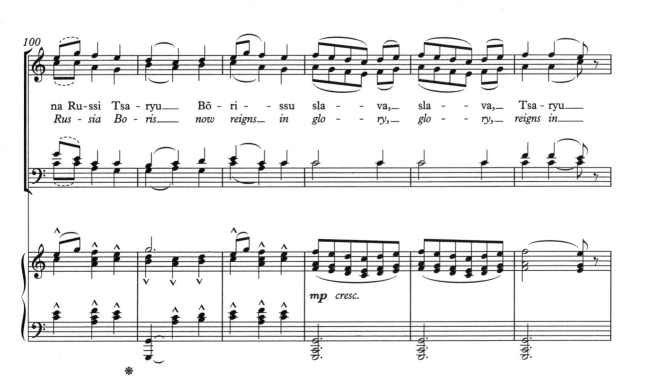

na Ru-ssi Tsa - ryu___ Bŏ - ri - - ssu sla - - va, sla - - va, Tsa - ryu___
*Rus - sia Bo - ris___ now reigns___ in glo - - ry, glo - - ry,___ reigns in___*

# 14. Humming chorus

(from *Madama Butterfly*)

GIACOMO PUCCINI
(1858–1924)

# 15. Dido's lament, and final chorus

(from *Dido and Aeneas*)

Text by Nahum Tate

HENRY PURCELL
(1659–95)

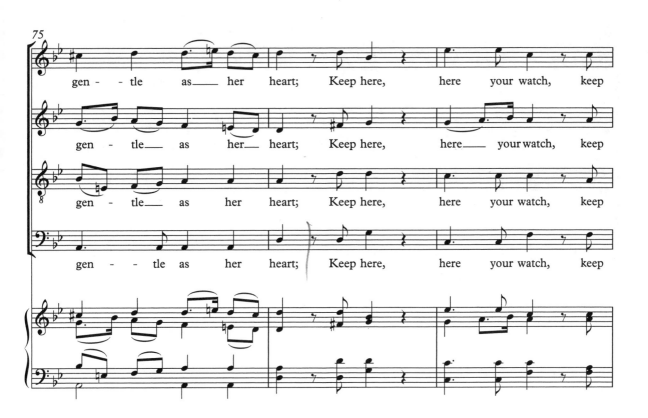

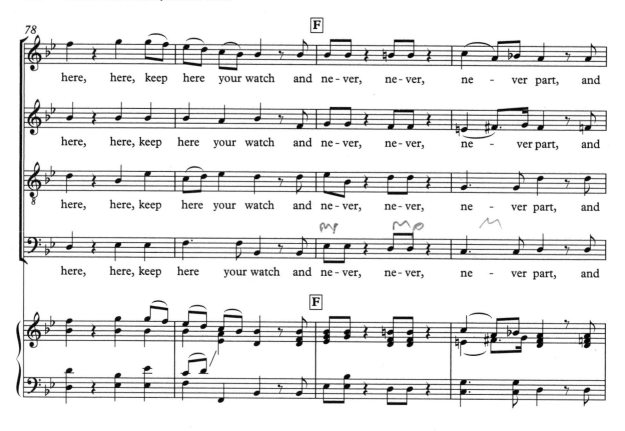

here, here, keep here your watch and ne-ver, ne-ver, ne - ver part, and
here, here, keep here your watch and ne-ver, ne-ver, ne - ver part, and
here, here, keep here your watch and ne-ver, ne-ver, ne - ver part, and
here, here, keep here your watch and ne-ver, ne-ver, ne - ver part, and

ne - ver, ne - ver, ne - ver, ne - ver part. With droop - part.
ne - ver, ne - ver, ne - ver, ne - ver part. part.
ne - ver, ne - ver, ne - ver, ne - ver part. With part.
ne - ver, ne - ver, ne - ver, ne - ver part. part.

# 16. Procession of the nobles

(from *Mlada*)

Text after S. A. Gedeonov
tr. David Lloyd-Jones

NIKOLAI RIMSKY-KORSAKOV
(1844–1908)

**Allegro moderato e maestoso**

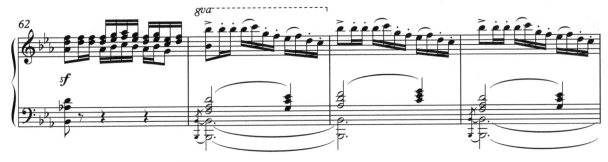

*The piano reduction is Rimsky-Korsakov's own.

# 17. Prayer

(from *Moïse*)

Text by L. Balocchi and E. de Jouy
tr. John Rutter

GIOACHINO ROSSINI
(1797–1868)

*This and the other solo sections can be sung by the chorus.

*In the absence of soloists, chorus sopranos may sing the solo soprano part from here to the end.

# 18. Villagers' chorus

(from *Guillaume Tell*)

Text by E. de Jouy and others, after Schiller
tr. John Rutter

GIOACHINO ROSSINI
(1792–1868)

Quel jour se - rein le ciel___ pré - sa - ge; Cé - lé - brons le___ dans
*Bright and se - rene the day___ is___ break - ing; Wel - come in song___ this*

nos___ con - certs! Que les é - chos de ce ri - va - ge É -
*morn___ so___ fair! Val - ley and hill soft e - choes mak - ing While*

# 19. Chorus of peasant girls

## (from *Eugene Onegin*)

Text by K. S. Shilovsky and the composer, after Pushkin
tr. David Lloyd-Jones

PIOTR TCHAIKOVSKY
(1840–93)

Dye - vi - tsyi, kras - sa - vi - tsyi,— du - shen - ki pŏ - dru - zhen - ki!
*Dear com - pan - ions, come this way,— join us in the games we play.*

nye khŏ-di pŏd-slu- -shi-vat(s), nye khŏ-di pŏd-sma- -tri-vat(s)
'Ne-ver come a-gain to spy on the girl-ish games we play,

nye khŏ-di pŏd-slu- -shi-vat(s), nye khŏ-di pŏd-sma- -tri-vat(s)
'Ne-ver come a-gain to spy on the girl-ish games we play,

i- -gryi na-shi dye- -vi- -chi!'
on the girl-ish games we play!'

i- -gryi na-shi dye- -vi- -chi!'
on the girl-ish games we play!'

# 20. Waltz scene

### (from *Eugene Onegin*)

Text by K. S. Shilovsky and the composer, after Pushkin
tr. David Lloyd-Jones

PIOTR TCHAIKOVSKY
(1840–93)

\* The piano reduction is Tchaikovsky's own.

Vot    tak    syur - priz,         ni - kak    nye o - zhi - da - li
*This     is    su - perb!*         *We    ne - - ver had ex - pect - ed*

*Bass Ds here may be meant to be Es.

* The section from here to bar 211 could be sung with sopranos taking 1st alto, altos taking 2nd alto (all impersonating the elderly ladies).

200 1st ALTOS        1st and 2nd ALTOS

zhal-ko Ta - nyu-shu! vŏz - myot ye - yov zho-nyi i bu-dyet ti - ra - -
*sad for Ta - tya - na, for once they are mar-ried She'll find he's a ty - - -*

cresc.

206       K

- nit(s)! On slyi - shno i - grok!
*-rant.* *He gam - bles, what's more!*

mf    p    ff

212

218

224    ALTOS *f*   L

On nye - uch strash - nyi, su - mas -
*He's most dis - court - eous and con -*

*f*

\*This cut is intended only for performances without soloists.

* See note to bar 69.

# 21. Anvil chorus

(from *Il trovatore*)

Text by Salvatore Cammarano
tr. John Rutter

GIUSEPPE VERDI
(1813–1901)

# 22. Brindisi

(from *La traviata*)

Text by F. M. Piave
tr. John Rutter

GIUSEPPE VERDI
(1813–1901)

# 23. Chorus of the Hebrew slaves

(from *Nabucco*)

Text by T. Solera
tr. John Rutter

GIUSEPPE VERDI
(1813–1901)

Lyrics (measures 21–27):

-da — — no le ri — ve sa — lu — — ta,    Di Si-
stand  by__  the banks  of__ the Jor — — dan    And  to

-on — ne le tor — ri at-ter — ra — — te...    Oh  mia
see  Si — on's woe — ful de — so — la — — tion!    O  dear

pa — — tria sì bel — — la e per — du — — ta!    Oh  mem-
land,  once the joy  of  our na — tion,    Now  for-

-bran — za sì ca — ra e fa — tal!    Ar — pa
-ev — er lost  by Fate's  cru — el hand.    Gold — en

-vel - - la del tem - - po_ che fu! O si-
times now so long gone_ and past. O Je-

-mì - - le di So - - li - ma ai fa - - - - ti Trag - gi un
-ru - - -sa-lem, bless - ed ci - - - ty, When will

suo - - no di cru - - do la-men - - to, O t'i-
grief and la - ment - ing be o - - ver? Let our

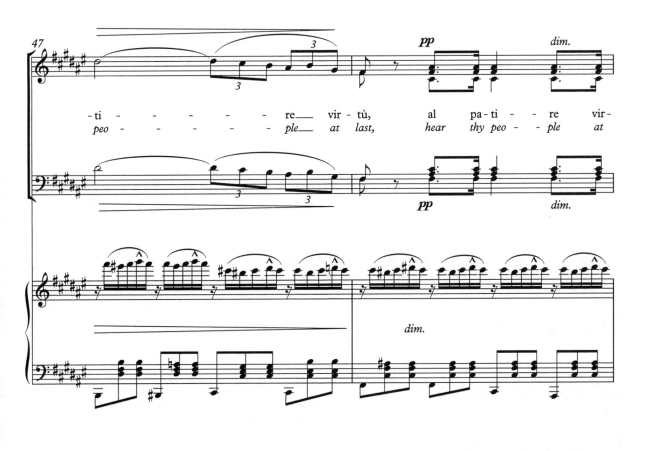

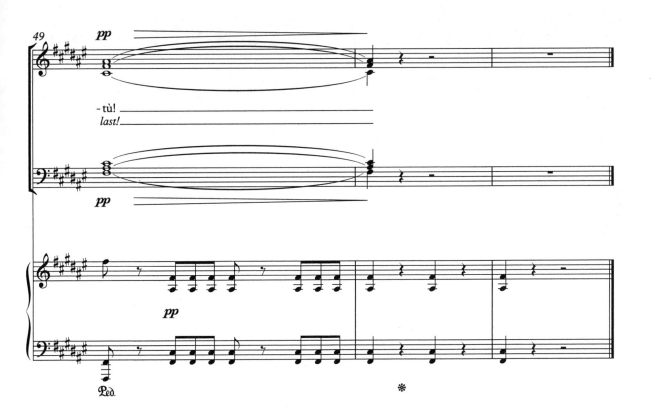

# 24. Chorus of Scottish refugees

(from *Macbeth*)

Text by F. M. Piave, after Shakespeare
tr. John Rutter

GIUSEPPE VERDI
(1813–1901)

# 25. Matadors' chorus

(from *La traviata*)

Text by F. M. Piave
tr. John Rutter

GIUSEPPE VERDI
(1813–1901)

**Allegro assai mosso**

PIANO

*ff*

***TENORS and BASSES**

unis. *f*

Di Ma - dri - de noi siam mat - ta - do - ri, sia - mo i pro - di del cir - co dei
We are fear - less and bold ma - ta - do - ri, Gal - lant he - roes of le - gend and

[*f*]

to - ri, te - stè giun - ti a go - de - re del chias - so che a Pa - ri - gi si fa pel Bue
sto - ry; Just ar - rived from Ma - drid, we are rea - dy For Pa - ree, where the plea - sures are

**A**

gras - so; è u - na sto - ria, se u - di - re vor - re - te, qua - li a - man - ti noi sia - mo, sa -
hea - dy; We've a sto - ry in which you'll dis - co - ver In - spi - ra - tion for ev - 'ry young

*p*

★Tenor solo (Gastone) sings in unison with 1st tenors throughout this chorus.

© Oxford University Press 1995.  Photocopying copyright material is illegal.

*In performances without soloists, omit these bracketed voice parts; they should not be sung by chorus tenors and basses.

* pronounce as two syllables: 'fy-ah'

Text underlay:

58
-ne___ par - lò:          Cin - - que    to - ri in un sol gior - no
young___ girl said:      'Five    bulls  slain in one day___ would show me

66
vo' ve - der - ti ad at - ter - rar;    e,  se vin - ci, al tuo ri - tor - no
You  can  tru - ly  play___ your part;  On - ly then will I  let___ you know me,

74
ma - no e cor - ti vo' do - nar.    Sì,___ gli dis - se, e il mat - ta - do - re
I  shall give___ you all___ my heart.'  They___ a - greed, and  off___ he hur - ried,

SOPRANOS and ALTOS (+SOP. SOLO)

103

Bra — vo, bra-vo il mat-ta-do-re, ben ga-gliar-do si mo-strò,
*Bra — vo, bra-vo! how cou-ra-geous! One can sure-ly un-der-stand*

BARITONE and BASS SOLI

112

se al-la gio-vi-ne l'a-mo-re in tal gui-sa e-gli pro-vò!
*How ro-man-tic, yet how out-ra-geous Was the price of that beau-ty's hand!*

F

120

1st TENORS

Poi, tra plau-si, ri-tor-na-to al-la bel-la del suo cor,
*When the crowd had long ap-plaud-ed He re-turned to claim his bride;*

2nd TENORS

BASSES

F

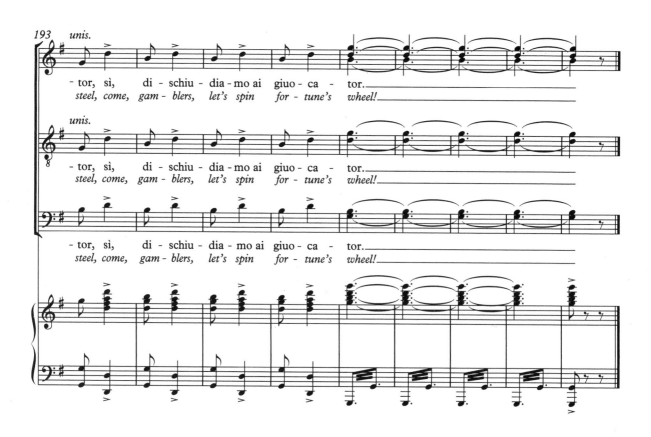

# 26. Rataplan

(from *La forza del destino*)

Text by F. M. Piave
tr. John Rutter

GIUSEPPE VERDI
(1813–1901)

Note: The chorus is offstage in bars 5–7, onstage by bar 20. In concert performance bars 5–7 could be sung softly to reproduce the effect.

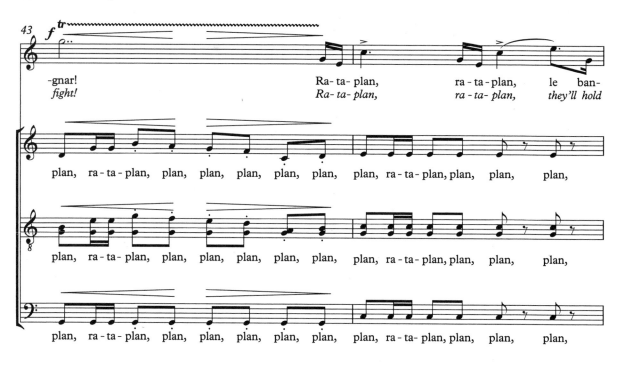

# 27. Soldiers' chorus

(from *Il trovatore*)

Text by S. Cammarano
tr. John Rutter

GIUSEPPE VERDI
(1813–1901)

# 28. Triumphal scene

(from *Aida*)

Text by Antonio Ghislanzoni
tr. John Rutter

GIUSEPPE VERDI
(1813–1901)

**Allegro maestoso** ( ♩ = 100 )

PIANO

**cresc. e string. a poco a poco**

**CHORUS OF PRIESTS**

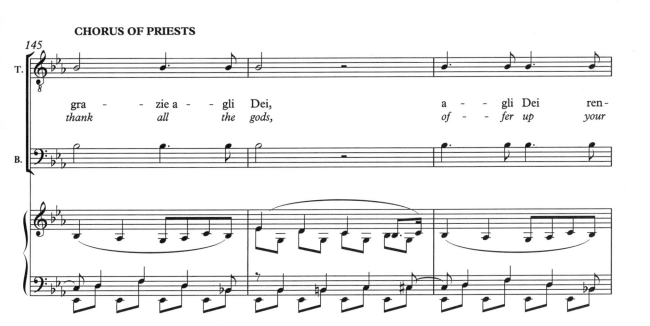

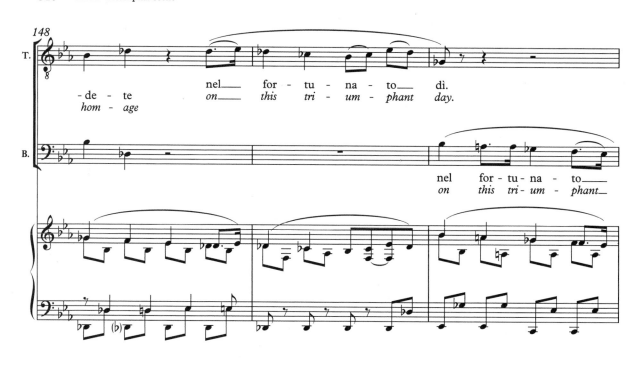

# 29. Witches' chorus

### (from *Macbeth*)

Text by F. M. Piave, after Shakespeare
tr. John Rutter

GIUSEPPE VERDI
(1813–1901)

* Verdi adds: 'Don't forget that these are witches who are speaking.'

# 30. Bridal chorus

(from *Lohengrin*)

Text by the composer
tr. John Rutter

RICHARD WAGNER
(1813–83)

**Mässig bewegt** [In moderate time]

Treu - lich ge - führt     zie - het da - hin,
*Led   here   in faith,     draw near with joy,*

wo euch der Se - gen der Lie - be be - wahr!     Sieg - rei - cher Mut,
*Love's guar - dian an - gel will watch o - ver you!     Joined   in   a   bond*

wo euch die Lie - - - be be - wahr!
*Love's guar - dian an - - gel o - ver you!*

Min - ne - ge - winn     eint euch in Treu - e zum se - lig - sten Paar.
*none   can   de - stroy;     Now   you   are one in your love e - ver true.*

Strei - ter der Tu - gend, schrei - te vor - an!
*Vir - tue's brave cham - pion, step forth with pride!*

Zier - de der Ju - gend,
*Youth's fair - est flo - wer,*

schrei - te vor - an!
*walk by his side!*

Rau - schen des Fe - stes— seid— nun ent - ron - nen,
*Sounds of the feast - ing— now— left be - hind you,*

schrei - te vor - an!
*walk by his side!*

Dem Fe — ste seid ent - ron - nen,
*The feast — ing left be - hind you,*

Won - ne des Her - zens sei euch ge - won - nen!
*May joy and bliss be wait - ing to find you!*

Duf - ten - der Raum, zur
*Fra - grant and bright, this*

*This direction is the composer's, but the passage can be sung by all sopranos and altos.

**Im ersten Zeitmass** [Tempo I]

Treu - lich be - wacht    blei - bet zu - rück    wo  euch  der Se - gen der
*Du - ty  is  done;*    *now  we  de - part.*    *Love's  guar - dian an - gel  give*

wo  euch  die Lie - - -
*Love's  guar - dian an - - -*

Lie - be be - wahr!    Sieg - rei - cher Mut,    Min - ne  und Glück
*bless - ing  to  you.*    *Joy  in  your life,*    *bliss  in  your heart,*

- - be be - wahr!
- - gel  to  you.

# 31. Pilgrims' chorus

(from *Tannhäuser*)

Text by the composer
tr. John Rutter

RICHARD WAGNER
(1813–83)

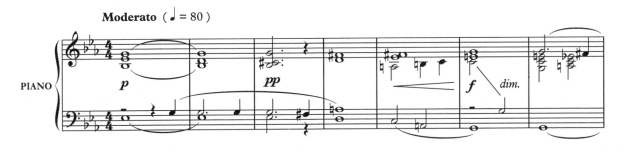

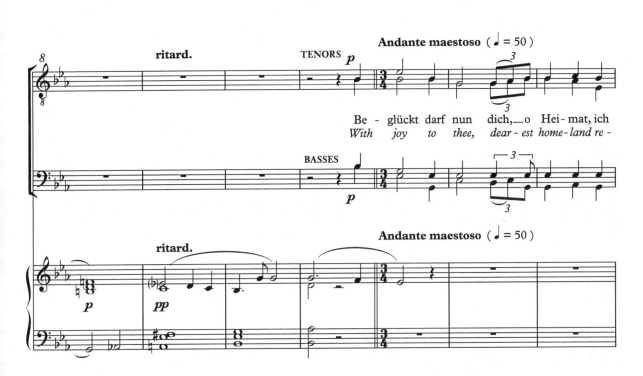

Wan - der - stab, weil Gott___ ge - treu ich ge - pil - - gert hab'.
*lay___ to rest, My vows___ ful - filled,___ my jour - - ney blest.*

Durch Sühn'___ und___ Buss'___ hab'
*Re - pen - tance___ have___ I___*

ich___ ver - söhnt___ den Her - ren,___ dem mein Her - ze___ fröhnt, der
*shown___ to God,___ My___ strength___ through all___ the lands I___ trod;___ Now*

# 32. Procession and chorale

(from *Die Meistersinger von Nürnberg*)

Text by the composer
tr. John Rutter

RICHARD WAGNER
(1813–83)

*From here to the start of bar 71 the chorus part is marked to be sung by the apprentices; from there to bar 77 by the crowd; the chorale by all including the mastersingers; bar 95 onwards by the crowd excluding the mastersingers.

†If preferred, sing this phrase in the original Latin.

*Composer's note: The fermata to be very long, and sustained evenly and strongly.

# 33. Sailors' chorus

(from *Der fliegende Holländer*)

Text by the composer
tr. John Rutter

RICHARD WAGNER
(1813–83)

Steu-er-mann, lass'_____ die Wacht! Steu-er-mann, her_____ zu uns! Ho!___ He!___
*Sai-lor-man, leave_____ your watch! Sai-lor-man, join_____ our throng! Yo___ ho!___*

Komm', lass' die Wacht! Komm' her zu uns!
*Come leave your watch! Come join our throng!*

Je!_____ Ha! Hisst die Se-gel auf! An-ker fest! Steu-er-mann, her!
*Yo_____ ho! Tie the an-chor rope tight-ly and hur-ry a - long!*

# 34. Spinning chorus

(from *Der fliegende Holländer*)

Text by the composer
tr. John Rutter

RICHARD WAGNER
(1813–83)

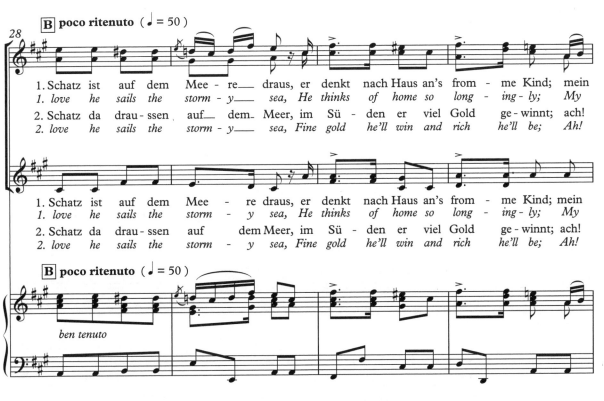

# 35. Huntsmen's chorus

(from *Der Freischütz*)

Text by Friedrich Kind
tr. John Rutter

C. M. von WEBER
(1786–1826)

Fel - sen uns hal - lend__ um - fan - gen, tönt frei - er und freud' - ger der
*moun - tain so loft - y__ a - round us, The wine cup will flow and right*

TENORS

4 or 8 SOLO VOICES    la    la    la

BASSES

vol - le Po - kal!    Jo    ho    tra la la la la la    la    la la la    la la la    la la la la    la la
*mer - - ry we'll feel!*

unis.

scherzando

la la   la la   la la la la   la la la la   la la la la la la   la!

la la la la la la la la la la   la la la la la la   la la la la la la   la!

# INDEX OF VOCAL AND INSTRUMENTAL REQUIREMENTS

Notes:
1. In the orchestral rental scores and parts, parts for clarinet in C are shown for normal B flat clarinet, all horn parts for horn in F, and all trumpet parts for B flat or, in certain cases, C trumpet.
2. ( ) denotes an optional voice or instrument.
3. Divisions within each choral voice-part have not been noted unless they are consistent throughout a chorus.

1. **Beethoven: Prisoners' chorus**
   Tenor solo or semi-chorus; bass solo; chorus TTBB
   2fl, 2ob, 2cl, 2bsn, 2hn, 2tpt, str
2. **Berlioz: Roman carnival**
   Soprano solo; semi-chorus of 3 tenors, 3 basses; chorus SATB. Picc, fl, 2ob, 2cl, 2bsn, 4hn, 2cornets [or tpts], 2tpt, 3tbn, tba [orig. ophicleide], timp, perc, str
3. **Bizet: Habanera**
   Mezzo-soprano solo; chorus SATB. 2fl, 2ob, 2cl, 2bsn, 4hn, (2tpt), (timp), perc, str
4. **Bizet: March of the toreadors**
   Children's chorus [unis.]; chorus SATB. Picc, fl, 2ob, 2cl, 2bsn, 4hn, 2tpt, 3tbn, timp, perc, str
5. **Borodin: Polovtsian dances**
   (Bass solo); chorus SATB. Picc, 2fl, 2ob [2nd doub. CA], 2cl, 2bsn, 4hn, 2tpt, 3tbn, tba, timp, perc, hp, str
6. **Donizetti: Chorus of wedding guests**
   Tenor solo; chorus SATB. Picc, 2fl, 2ob, 2cl, 2bsn, 4hn, 2tpt, 3tbn, timp, perc, str
7. **Gounod: Soldiers' chorus**
   Chorus TTBB. Picc, fl, 2ob, 2cl, 2bsn, 4hn, 2cornets [or tpts], 3tbn, timp, perc, str
8. **Handel: Chorus of enchanted islanders**
   Chorus SATB. 2ob, 2hn, (continuo), str
9. **Leoncavallo: Bell chorus**
   Chorus SATB. 3fl, 2ob, 2cl, (bass cl), 3bsn, 4hn, 3tpt, 3tbn, tba, timp, (bells), hp, str
10. **Mascagni: Easter hymn**
    Soprano solo; (alto solo); SATB double chorus. Picc, 2fl, 2ob, 2cl, 2bsn, 4hn, 2tpt, 3tbn, tba, timp, perc, organ, str
11. **Mozart: Priests' chorus**
    Chorus TTB. 2fl, 2ob, 2bsn, 2hn, 2tpt, 3tbn, str
12. **Mozart: Voyagers' chorus**
    Soprano solo; chorus SATB. 2fl, 2cl, 2hn, str
13. **Mussorgsky: Coronation scene**
    Tenor solo; bass solo; semi-chorus of basses; chorus SATB. Picc, 2fl, 2ob, 2cl, 2bsn, 4hn, 2tpt, 3tbn, tba, timp, perc, bells, pno duet, str
14. **Puccini: Humming chorus**
    Chorus of sopranos and tenors only.
    3fl, 2cl, bass cl, hn, hp, str, (solo viola d'amore)
15. **Purcell: Dido's lament, and final chorus**
    Mezzo-soprano solo; chorus SATB. Str, continuo
16. **Rimsky-Korsakov: Procession of the nobles**
    Chorus SATB. Picc, 3fl, 2ob, CA, 3cl, bass cl, 2bsn, c-bsn, 6hn, 3tpt, 3tbn, timp, perc, hp, str
17. **Rossini: Prayer**
    (Soprano or mezzo-soprano, tenor, and bass soli); chorus SATB. 2fl, 2ob, 2cl, 2bsn, 2hn, 2tpt, 3tbn, tba [orig. ophicleide], timp, perc, hp, str

18. **Rossini: Villagers' chorus**
    Chorus SATB. 2fl, 2ob, 2cl, 2bsn, 2hn, 2tpt, 3tbn, timp, str
19. **Tchaikovsky: Chorus of peasant girls**
    Chorus SSA. 2fl, 2ob, 2cl, 2bsn, 4hn, str
20. **Tchaikovsky: Waltz scene**
    (Tenor solo, baritone solo, bass solo); chorus SATB. Picc, 2fl, 2ob, 2cl, 2bsn, 4hn, 2tpt, 3tbn, timp, str
21. **Verdi: Anvil chorus**
    Chorus SATB. Picc, fl, 2ob, 2cl, 2bsn, 4hn, 2tpt, 3tbn, tba [orig. cimbasso], timp, perc, str
22. **Verdi: Brindisi**
    Soprano solo; tenor solo; chorus SATB. Orchestra as for no. 21
23. **Verdi: Chorus of the Hebrew slaves**
    Chorus SATB. Orchestra as for no. 21
24. **Verdi: Chorus of Scottish refugees**
    Chorus SATTB. Orchestra as for no. 21
25. **Verdi: Matadors' chorus**
    (Soprano, tenor, baritone, and bass soli); chorus SATB. Orchestra as for no. 21
26. **Verdi: Rataplan**
    Mezzo-soprano solo [required to sing top C]; chorus SATB. Orchestra as for no. 21
27. **Verdi: Soldiers' chorus**
    Chorus TB. Orchestra as for no. 21
28. **Verdi: Triumphal scene**
    Double chorus SATB: TTBB. Picc, fl, 2ob, 2cl, 2bsn, 4hn, 3tpt, 3tbn, tba [orig. cimbasso], timp, perc, str, (Egyptian tpts 1,2,3 in A flat, playing in unison; Egyptian tpts 4,5,6 in B, playing in unison, all cued into orchestral tpt. parts)
29. **Verdi: Witches' chorus**
    Chorus SSA. Picc, 2fl, 2ob, 2cl, 2bsn, 4hn, 2tpt, 3tbn, b.tbn [or tba], timp, perc, str
30. **Wagner: Bridal chorus**
    Chorus SATB; (semi-chorus of 4 sopranos and 4 altos). 3fl, 2ob, 2cl, 3bsn, 4hn, 2tpt, 3tbn, tba, perc, hp, str
31. **Wagner: Pilgrims' chorus**
    Chorus TTBB. 2fl, 2ob, 2cl, 2bsn, 4hn, 3tbn, tba, timp, str
32. **Wagner: Procession and chorale**
    Chorus SATB. Picc, 2fl, 2ob, 2cl, 2bsn, 4hn, 3tpt, 3tbn, tba, timp, perc, str, (on-stage tpt and drum, cued into orchestra)
33. **Wagner: Sailors' chorus**
    Chorus TTBB. Picc, 2fl, 2ob, 2cl, 2bsn, 4hn, 2tpt, 3tbn, tba, timp, str
34. **Wagner: Spinning chorus**
    Chorus SA. 2fl, 2ob, 2cl, 2bsn, 4hn, str
35. **Weber: Huntsmen's chorus**
    Chorus TTBB; semi-chorus TTBB. 2fl, 2ob, 2cl, 2bsn, 4hn, 2tpt, tbn, timp, str